TIMELINE OF JOHANN SEBASTIAN BACH'S LIFE

1685 Johann Sebastian Bach is born in Eisenach. His father is a musician and director of musical events there.

1694 Sebastian's mother dies, and his father dies the next year. Sebastian moves in with his older brother, Christoph, who lives in Ohrdruf.

1696 Sebastian learns to play the organ and sings in the school choir.

1700 Sebastian goes to Lüneburg to attend school. He supports himself by singing in the church choir.

1703 Sebastian becomes organist at a church in Arnstadt.

1705 Bach visits Lübeck to meet the great church organist Dietrich Buxtehude.

1707 Bach takes a job as an organist in Mühlhausen. He marries Maria Barbara Bach, a musician.

1708 Bach becomes organist and violinist in the Duke of Weimar's court.

THIS WAY

1714 Bach is appointed concert master in Weimar.

1717 Bach and Duke Wilhelm Ernst have a big disagreement, and Bach is thrown in prison for a month. He then leaves Weimar to take a job as music directer in Köthen.

1720 Sebastian's wife dies.

1721 Bach marries Anna Magdalena Wilcken.

1723 Bach is placed in charge of music events at St. Thomas's Church in Leipzig.

1729 J. S. Bach becomes director of the Collegium Musicum. This group performs in local coffee houses, allowing regular people to hear great music.

1736 Bach is appointed Royal Court Composer.

1737 -1749 J. S. Bach continues to write many important works, including pieces for students.

1750 Johann Sebastian Bach dies in Leipzig, Germany.

UP HERE

GETTING TO KNOW
THE WORLD'S
GREATEST COMPOSERS

JOHANN SEBASTIAN
BACH

WRITTEN AND ILLUSTRATED BY MIKE VENEZIA

CONSULTANT
DONALD FREUND, PROFESSOR OF COMPOSITION,
INDIANA UNIVERSITY SCHOOL OF MUSIC

CHILDREN'S PRESS®

An Imprint of Scholastic Inc.

A special thanks to the Music Department at Grace Lutheran Church and School in River Forest, Illinois, especially Dr. Richard Hillert and Mr. John Folkening.

Photos ©: cover and title page: Stock Montage; 3: akg-images; 6 top: Copyright of the image Museo Nacional del Prado/Art Resource, NY; 6 bottom: Erich Lessing/Art Resource, NY; 8: Scala/Art Resource, NY; 9: bpk Bildagentur/Mendelssohn-Archiv, Staatsbibliothek, Berlin/ Carola Seifert/Art Resource, NY; 10: SLUB Dresden/Deutsche Fotothek; 14 left: Bettmann/ Getty Images; 14 right: DEA/G. P. Cavallero/Getty Images; 18, 20: akg-images; 21: The Pierpont Morgan Library, Mary Flagler Cary Music Collection/Art Resource, NY; 24-25, 25 bottom, 27 all, 30, 31: akg-images; 32: Bettmann/Getty Images; 33-35: Stock Montage.

Library of Congress Cataloging-in-Publication Data

Names: Venezia, Mike, author, illustrator.
Title: Johann Sebastian Bach / written and illustrated by Mike Venezia.
Description: Revised edition. | New York : Children's Press, 2017. | Series:
  Getting to know the world's greatest composers | Includes index.
Identifiers: LCCN 2016045688| ISBN 9780531220603 (library binding) |
  ISBN 9780531222423 (pbk.)
Subjects: LCSH: Bach, Johann Sebastian, 1685-1750—Juvenile literature. |
  Composers—Germany—Biography—Juvenile literature.
Classification: LCC ML3930.B2 V46 2017 | DDC 780.92 [B] —dc23 LC record available at
https://lccn.loc.gov/2016045688

Scholastic Inc., 557 Broadway, New York, NY 10012.

6 7 8 9 10 11 R 27 26 25 24 23

A portrait of Johann Sebastian Bach as a young man

Johann Sebastian Bach was born in the German town of Eisenach in 1685. During his lifetime, J. S. Bach was known more as a great harpsichord player and organist than as a composer. Most of the beautiful music he wrote didn't become popular until many years after he died.

Johann Sebastian Bach came from a large family of musicians. More than seventy of his uncles, cousins, brothers, and other relatives made their livings as musicians, choirmasters, and composers. There were so many musical Bachs in Germany that in some areas, being a

Bach meant the same thing as being a musician.
  Every year, members of the Bach family got together for a reunion. They had a great time playing their favorite music and then making up funny songs that kept them laughing for hours.

Johann Sebastian Bach played and composed his music during a time known as the Baroque period. In the 1600s and 1700s, everything in Europe seemed to have a grand, fancy, and decorative feeling to it. Art and architecture were created to show off the palaces and homes of kings, queens, dukes, and wealthy businessmen.

A painting by Baroque artist Peter Paul Rubens (above) and a stairway inside a Baroque German palace (left)

Baroque music also had kind of a grand, decorative feeling. It was often filled with the sounds of voices, violins, trumpets, and flutes, each playing different melodies at the same time. J. S. Bach was an expert at making complicated Baroque pieces sound natural and pleasing.

Wealthy people would listen to their favorite Baroque music at royal court gatherings or at the opera. Regular everyday people could hear wonderful choral and organ music in their local churches.

Musicians playing during a European court gathering in the early 1700s

Johann Ambrosius Bach, the father of Johann Sebastian Bach

Town musicians often played at celebrations and special events. J. S. Bach's father was a town musician. He probably taught his son to play the violin and introduced him to other instruments.

When J. S. Bach (who was usually called Sebastian) was nine years old, a very sad thing happened—his mother died. Then, only a year later, his father died, too.

A sad Sebastian Bach went to live with his older brother, Christoph, in the nearby town of Ohrdruf. Christoph Bach was known as an excellent church organist. He not only taught Sebastian to play the harpsichord and organ, but how to tune and fix broken organs.

Organs being built and repaired in the early 1700s

Johann Sebastian Bach tested and repaired
organs in different towns around Germany.
It was one of the ways he made extra money
throughout his life.

When Sebastian was fifteen years old, he left his brother's home to look for a job. He traveled two hundred miles on foot to the town of Lüneburg. There he attended school and became a member of the church choir.

This was the beginning of many trips Sebastian would take during his life. He was always looking for the best music job he could get. Sometimes, his music jobs came along with chores that weren't very pleasant. When he was seventeen years old, Sebastian got a great job as a violinist in the royal court at Celle, Germany. But as part of the job, he also had to remove slop from the kitchen every morning!

As he moved to different towns, working as a choirmaster (a person who leads a choir), musician, or church organist, J. S. Bach learned more and more about music.

A 17th-century organist (left) and a photograph of one of the organs played by Bach (above)

Johann Sebastian Bach took side trips, too. He wanted to listen to well-known organists and composers to get ideas for his own music. On one trip, he heard a famous organist named Dietrich Buxtehude play. Sebastian was inspired by Buxtehude's animated and imaginative music. Soon Sebastian started creating new and exciting music in his own style.

One of Bach's most famous organ
compositions during this time is called
Toccata and Fugue in D Minor. This piece
is filled with big, powerful sounds. It had an
energy and force that had never been heard
before. Many of J. S. Bach's mighty organ
pieces have been known to cause church
rafters and windows to shake!

Johann Sebastian Bach was a very religious person. He belonged to the Lutheran Church. One important type of musical piece he wrote for church services is called a cantata. A cantata features voices. It usually has a lead singer and a choir accompanied by an orchestra. J. S. Bach wrote hundreds of cantatas. In each one you can feel his love for God. These beautiful works were a very important part of the Lutheran church service.

Bach's cantatas usually included hymn tunes, called chorales, that most people knew and loved.

In J. S. Bach's time, a church service could last for five hours or more! People depended on cantata music to keep them interested and awake.

Weimar as it looked during Bach's time

It wasn't long before J. S. Bach became well known for his remarkable talent as an organist and composer of church music. This made it easier for him to find better jobs. When Sebastian was working as an organist in the town of Mühlhausen, he met and fell in love with Maria Barbara Bach, a distant cousin. They got married, and Maria was happy to travel around with her husband and raise their family.

In 1708, Sebastian got an excellent job in the court of Duke Wilhelm Ernst of Saxe-Weimar. Bach wrote some of his most important organ works there. Unfortunately, after several years, Sebastian felt the duke was becoming too bossy. He decided to take a new job at a friendlier court. When the duke heard about Bach's decision, he became angry and had Johann Sebastian Bach thrown in jail for a whole month!

Being in jail was a very depressing experience for Johann Sebastian Bach. He couldn't wait to get out and start his new job with Prince Leopold of Köthen, Germany.

Sebastian and the prince got along really well. Sebastian composed mainly instrumental music for the prince. He also wrote the first book of *The Well-Tempered Clavier*, and *The Little Organ Book*. These keyboard works are still played by music students today.

After three happy years in Prince Leopold's court, things quickly changed for the worse. First, Sebastian's wife, Maria, died. Then the prince got married, and his new wife didn't care for music at all.

Prince Leopold of Köthen

A page from an original handwritten piece of music by J. S. Bach

Soon, the prince started losing interest in music, too. Sebastian felt it was time to move on and look for a new job again.

efore he left Prince Leopold's court, J. S. Bach wrote a set of his most famous and popular works—the *Brandenburg Concertos*. A concerto is a musical piece in which one instrument, or a small group of instruments, stands out from the rest of the orchestra. It's a good way for an excellent musician to show off his or her talent. In the *Brandenburg Concertos*, trumpets, violins, oboes, flutes, harpsichords, or cellos play along with a larger orchestra to make up some of the best "feeling-happy" music ever.

If you are in a grouchy or sad mood, these concertos are almost guaranteed to make you feel better. The *Brandenburg Concertos* are filled with beautiful musical sounds that are sometimes relaxing and peaceful, and sometimes bursting with joy. You can almost imagine yourself being at a royal event in some duke or king's palace when you listen to these pieces.

In 1723, J. S. Bach accepted a job as director of music in the historic city of Leipzig, Germany. This was probably Sebastian's busiest time. He was responsible for composing and directing music for four churches, a school choir, a university choir, and any music the city might need for special events.

Sebastian had remarried in 1721. His new wife's name was Anna Magdalena. Anna Magdalena and Sebastian ended up having thirteen children. With four children from his first marriage, Sebastian was very busy taking care of a large family.

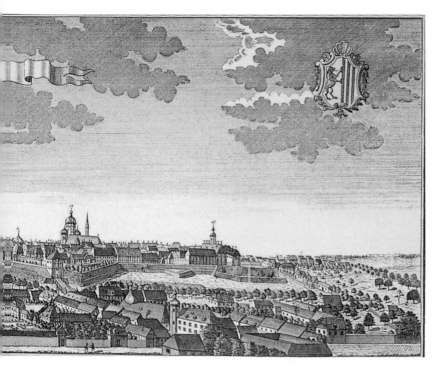

In 1723, Bach became
Director of Church Music
for the city of Leipzig,
Germany.

Johann Sebastian Bach and his family

One of the many things Sebastian had to do every week was to write down and make copies of the music he had written for all the choir and orchestra members. This was a really boring job, but Anna Magdalena and their children would often help out. As busy as he was, J. S. Bach always found time for his large family.

Wilhelm Friedemann Bach

Johann Christian Bach

He was a loving father and made sure all his children got good grades, learned to play musical instruments, and helped out around the house. Four of Bach's sons became famous composers and musicians.

C. P. E. Bach

Johann Christoph Friedrich Bach

Johann Sebastian Bach spent twenty-seven years in Leipzig. He composed some of his greatest works there, including the *Goldberg Variations*. These keyboard pieces take you on an amazing sound trip. They start out peacefully, build to a swirling musical whirlwind, and drop you back off where things are nice and calm again.

Another piece from this time, the *St. Matthew Passion*, is filled with heavenly sounds and shows how Bach could put his deepest religious feelings into a work. And the joyful *Christmas Oratorio* has some of the biggest and cheeriest trumpet and horn sounds you'll ever hear!

Late in J. S. Bach's life, musical tastes
began to change. People were growing tired
of what they thought were big, complicated
Baroque sounds. They wanted music that
was simpler and lighter. Bach heard some of
the latest music of the day in coffee houses
around Leipzig, where college students and
musicians traveling through town sometimes
played popular new music.

The Thomaskirche, one of the four churches Bach directed music for in Leipzig

*E*ven though Johann Sebastian Bach knew things were changing musically, he decided to stick with his favorite Baroque style. Some people criticized him for being old-fashioned. In Leipzig, it seemed like Bach was always being given a hard time, especially from his bosses. J. S. Bach had dozens of bosses. Most of them had very little understanding of music.

Bach always had trouble getting raises or money for necessary music equipment. Members of the town council thought Sebastian wasn't working hard enough. The principal of the church school thought music was a waste of time for his students. And the head of the university thought Bach was directing the choir poorly!

A statue of Johann Sebastian Bach in front of the Thomaskirche in Leipzig

A portrait of Johann Sebastian Bach holding a piece of his own music

Johann Sebastian Bach always stood up for his rights, though. He often ignored silly complaints. When he died in 1750, he had composed some of the world's most beautiful music ever, whether his bosses liked it or not!

It's easy to hear Bach's great music. You can go online and stream his music for free. Also, many neighborhood churches put on free Bach concerts throughout the year.

LEARN MORE BY TAKING THE BACH QUIZ!

(ANSWERS ON THE NEXT PAGE.)

1. J. S. Bach was a super-talented organ player. The large church organs he played needed huge amounts of air blowing through their pipes to make powerful musical sounds. How was the airflow generated?
- a. Dozens of wiener dogs ran on treadmills, powering huge fans to create airflow.
- b. Organists had to wait for a severe windstorm and "capture" air in large balloons to supply the organ.
- c. Workers would pump large bellows to feed air into the organ system.

2. For hundreds of years, Germany has been famous for its many delicious types of sausages. What were some popular sausage dishes Sebastian Bach might have enjoyed?
- a. Hot dogs with sauerkraut
- b. Thuringers and dumplings
- c. Hot Italian sausage with peppers on crusty bread

3. As a young conductor, J. S. Bach got into a major fight with a bassoon player named Johann Heinrich Geyersbach. What were the men fighting about?
- a. Geyersbach said bassoons were 100 times cooler than pipe organs.
- b. Bach said pipe organs were 1,000 times cooler than bassoons.
- c. Sebastian insulted Geyersbach's playing ability.

4. TRUE OR FALSE: Harpsichord and clavichord are just old-fashioned names for the piano.

5. TRUE OR FALSE: J. S. Bach was so crazy about coffee, he wrote a major piece about the beverage using singers and a full orchestra.

33

ANSWERS

1. **c** Helpers worked out of sight behind the organ, pumping large bellows. Air from the bellows would build up in a wind chest and supply air to the organ pipes. Today, modern pipe organs use electric blowers to generate airflow.

2. **a & b** For a while, Sebastian lived near Frankfurt, where the frankfurter was invented. Today, the frankfurter is better known as the hot dog. He also lived in a region called Thuringia, where Thuringer sausages were invented. J. S. Bach probably enjoyed both of these delicious sausages with sauerkraut and dumplings on the side.

3. **c** Sebastian Bach insulted Johann Geyersbach by saying his bassoon playing sounded like a crying nanny goat. Later, the angry bassoonist attacked Bach in the town square. Fortunately, townspeople broke up the fight before either man was seriously hurt.

4. **FALSE** All three are keyboard instruments. The difference is harpsichord strings are plucked by prongs, which make a quick, bright sound. A clavichord is a smaller instrument. Its strings are struck by a metal blade, which give it a quieter, gentle sound. The piano was a newer instrument in Bach's day. Piano strings are struck by a felt-covered hammer that bounces back and allows the strings to continue vibrating for a louder, fuller sound.

5. **TRUE** When J. S. Bach was older, coffee was just becoming a popular drink in Germany. People loved going to coffee houses to listen to music while sipping their favorite beverage. Sebastian wrote a fun piece about the coffee craze, called the *Coffee Cantata*.